WHY CATS PAINT

Address Book

HEATHER BUSCH & BURTON SILVER

Ten Speed Press
Berkeley, California

WHY CATS PAINT

Nobody fully understands why some cats make marks with paint, but the phenomenon has been known for centuries, with the earliest recorded examples of cat marking dating back to Ancient Egypt.

In recent times, cat painting has been explained by biologists as being a form of territorial marking behavior, yet mounting evidence suggests that some cats' marks are aesthetically motivated and should be regarded as genuine works of non-primate art. Already there are several galleries, like the *Phillip Wood Gallery* in Berkeley, California, and *Villa Ichon* in Bremen, Germany, which specialize in the collection, curation and exhibition of cat art, and scientific publications such as the *American Journal of Non-Primate Art* regularly feature articles on feline aesthetics.

While all domestic cats undoubtedly have the ability to make aesthetically meaningful marks, and often display a creative ability with their claws, very few ever become skilled exponents with palette and paw. This has a lot to do with our limited human understanding of cats and our consequent reluctance to encourage them to undertake more complex tasks. So, while the internationally recognized cat artists featured in this book are most unusual, it must be remembered that all cats are potential artists and, provided they can be supplied with non-toxic, scented acrylic paints and access to suitable surfaces, a significant number may well surprise their owners with interesting work.

Almost all the contemporary works selected for this address book have been given a title either by the cat's owner or its curator. The reason for this is straightforward. Just as surrounding a painting with an expensive frame and hanging it in a gallery places a value on it, so, too, naming a work confirms artistic intent and allows the work to be legitimated and taken seriously.

Certainly, by titling a cat's painting, we provide a context within which judgements of aesthetic worth are made. A title such as *Fluff and Kittens* is likely to suggest a different level of worth than *Maternal Arrangements* or *Coital Consequences#4*. Nevertheless titles provide a clue, a starting point, no matter how arbitrary or contextually biased, from which to begin our journey of discovery into the fascinating world of feline creativity. Without them, we run the risk of dismissing cat painting as being no more relevant than the mindless territorial daubing of the graffitist.

Burton Silver and Heather Busch, 1996

Reindeer in Provence, (detail), 1992.
Acrylic on gold card and wall, 120 x 80cm.
Private collection, Paris.

MINNIE (Minnie Monet Manet), lives in Provence where she is well known for her advanced horizontal motifs.

A

NAME:

ADDRESS:

PHONE:

NAME:

ADDRESS:

PHONE:

NAME:

ADDRESS:

PHONE:

NAME:

ADDRESS:

PHONE:

NAME:

ADDRESS:

PHONE:

NAME:

ADDRESS:

PHONE:

NAME:

ADDRESS:

PHONE:

NAME:

ADDRESS:

PHONE:

NAME:

ADDRESS:

PHONE:

NAME:

ADDRESS:

PHONE:

A

NAME:

ADDRESS:

PHONE:

NAME:

ADDRESS:

PHONE:

NAME:

ADDRESS:

PHONE:

NAME:

ADDRESS:

PHONE:

NAME:

ADDRESS:

PHONE:

PUSCHEL, a four-year-old Ginger Tom, perfectly captures
the disparate nature of a spectacular avian banquet.

B

NAME:

ADDRESS:

PHONE:

NAME:

ADDRESS:

PHONE:

NAME:

ADDRESS:

PHONE:

NAME:

ADDRESS:

PHONE:

Feather Feast, (detail), 1995.
Acrylic on card, 76 x 45 cm.
Wissenschaftliches Institut für Forschung
in die Schönen Katzenkünste, Bremen.

NAME:

ADDRESS:

PHONE:

NAME:

ADDRESS:

PHONE:

NAME:

ADDRESS:

PHONE:

NAME:

ADDRESS:

PHONE:

NAME:

ADDRESS:

PHONE:

B

NAME:

ADDRESS:

PHONE:

NAME:

ADDRESS:

PHONE:

NAME:

ADDRESS:

PHONE:

NAME:

ADDRESS:

PHONE:

NAME:

ADDRESS:

PHONE:

NAME:

ADDRESS:

PHONE:

NAME:

ADDRESS:

PHONE:

NAME:

ADDRESS:

PHONE:

NAME:

ADDRESS:

PHONE:

NAME:

ADDRESS:

PHONE:

B

NAME:

ADDRESS:

PHONE:

NAME:

ADDRESS:

PHONE:

NAME:

ADDRESS:

PHONE:

NAME:

ADDRESS:

PHONE:

NAME:

ADDRESS:

PHONE:

GLOSSIP completed this evocative work after spending several days contemplating a neighbor's fish pond.

C

NAME:

ADDRESS:

PHONE:

NAME:

ADDRESS:

PHONE:

NAME:

ADDRESS:

PHONE:

NAME:

ADDRESS:

PHONE:

Fish Whispers, 1994.
Scented acrylic on blue card, 87 x 51cm.
Jane Prisletine Feline Art Trust, Sydney, Australia.

NAME:

ADDRESS:

PHONE:

NAME:

ADDRESS:

PHONE:

NAME:

ADDRESS:

PHONE:

NAME:

ADDRESS:

PHONE:

NAME:

ADDRESS:

PHONE:

C

NAME:

ADDRESS:

PHONE:

NAME:

ADDRESS:

PHONE:

NAME:

ADDRESS:

PHONE:

NAME:

ADDRESS:

PHONE:

NAME:

ADDRESS:

PHONE:

NAME:

ADDRESS:

PHONE:

NAME:

ADDRESS:

PHONE:

NAME:

ADDRESS:

PHONE:

NAME:

ADDRESS:

PHONE:

NAME:

ADDRESS:

PHONE:

C

NAME:

ADDRESS:

PHONE:

NAME:

ADDRESS:

PHONE:

NAME:

ADDRESS:

PHONE:

NAME:

ADDRESS:

PHONE:

NAME:

ADDRESS:

PHONE:

Little Mice Dance on the Tips of Their Tiny Claws No More, (detail), 1995.
Acrylic paste on colored card, 42 x 29.5 cm.
Private collection, Malibu, California.

Monty's intricate forms concentrate on the dichotomy between gastronomic indulgence and the delight of dance.

D

NAME: _____

ADDRESS: _____

_____

_____

PHONE: _____

NAME: _____

ADDRESS: _____

_____

_____

PHONE: _____

NAME: _____

ADDRESS: _____

_____

_____

PHONE: _____

NAME: _____

ADDRESS: _____

_____

_____

PHONE: _____

NAME: _____

ADDRESS: _____

_____

_____

PHONE: _____

NAME:

ADDRESS:

PHONE:

NAME:

ADDRESS:

PHONE:

NAME:

ADDRESS:

PHONE:

NAME:

ADDRESS:

PHONE:

NAME:

ADDRESS:

PHONE:

D

NAME:

ADDRESS:

PHONE:

NAME:

ADDRESS:

PHONE:

NAME:

ADDRESS:

PHONE:

NAME:

ADDRESS:

PHONE:

NAME:

ADDRESS:

PHONE:

PRINCESS, a Rex, specializes in finely crafted, classically minimalist scratch-forms on walls, doors and furniture.

E

NAME:

ADDRESS:

PHONE:

NAME:

ADDRESS:

PHONE:

NAME:

ADDRESS:

PHONE:

NAME:

ADDRESS:

PHONE:

Amongst the Pigeons, 1988.
Marks with claws on painted fiber-board
wall panel, 48 x 72cm.
Private collection, Chicago.

NAME:

ADDRESS:

PHONE:

NAME:

ADDRESS:

PHONE:

NAME:

ADDRESS:

PHONE:

NAME:

ADDRESS:

PHONE:

NAME:

ADDRESS:

PHONE:

E

NAME:

ADDRESS:

PHONE:

NAME:

ADDRESS:

PHONE:

NAME:

ADDRESS:

PHONE:

NAME:

ADDRESS:

PHONE:

NAME:

ADDRESS:

PHONE:

Experimental Insight, 1992.
Acrylic on colored board, 30 x 21cm.
Centre de recherche dans les
arts graphiques félins, Paris.

B<small>ITZ</small>'s technique is typified by enormous speed and energy which produces spontaneous works of great clarity.

F

NAME: _____

ADDRESS: _____

_____

_____

PHONE: _____

NAME: _____

ADDRESS: _____

_____

_____

PHONE: _____

NAME: _____

ADDRESS: _____

_____

_____

PHONE: _____

NAME: _____

ADDRESS: _____

_____

_____

PHONE: _____

NAME: _____

ADDRESS: _____

_____

_____

PHONE: _____

NAME:

ADDRESS:

PHONE:

NAME:

ADDRESS:

PHONE:

NAME:

ADDRESS:

PHONE:

NAME:

ADDRESS:

PHONE:

NAME:

ADDRESS:

PHONE:

F

NAME:

ADDRESS:

PHONE:

NAME:

ADDRESS:

PHONE:

NAME:

ADDRESS:

PHONE:

NAME:

ADDRESS:

PHONE:

NAME:

ADDRESS:

PHONE:

Cocking for Cockatoos, 1993.
Acrylic on card and plaster board wall, 110 x 95 cm.
Scraatchi Collection, London.

G

BOOTSIE is well known for the vigorous, sometimes quite aggressive style he uses to explore his inner feelings.

NAME:

ADDRESS:

PHONE:

NAME:

ADDRESS:

PHONE:

NAME:

ADDRESS:

PHONE:

NAME:

ADDRESS:

PHONE:

NAME:

ADDRESS:

PHONE:

NAME:

ADDRESS:

PHONE:

NAME:

ADDRESS:

PHONE:

NAME:

ADDRESS:

PHONE:

NAME:

ADDRESS.

PHONE:

NAME:

ADDRESS:

PHONE:

G

NAME:

ADDRESS:

PHONE:

NAME:

ADDRESS:

PHONE:

NAME:

ADDRESS:

PHONE:

NAME:

ADDRESS:

PHONE:

NAME:

ADDRESS:

PHONE:

NIKKI projects her secret longings on to raging forms which challenge with extravagant and licentious leaps.

H

NAME: _____

ADDRESS: _____

_____

_____

PHONE: _____

NAME: _____

ADDRESS: _____

_____

_____

PHONE: _____

NAME: _____

ADDRESS: _____

_____

_____

PHONE: _____

NAME: _____

ADDRESS: _____

_____

_____

PHONE: _____

Transcendental Tempest II, (detail), 1993.
Scented acrylic on colored card, 89 x 53cm.
Collection of the artist, Tokyo.

NAME:

ADDRESS:

PHONE:

NAME:

ADDRESS:

PHONE:

NAME:

ADDRESS:

PHONE:

NAME:

ADDRESS:

PHONE:

NAME:

ADDRESS:

PHONE:

H

NAME:

ADDRESS:

PHONE:

NAME:

ADDRESS:

PHONE:

NAME:

ADDRESS:

PHONE:

NAME:

ADDRESS:

PHONE:

NAME:

ADDRESS:

PHONE:

NAME:

ADDRESS:

PHONE:

NAME:

ADDRESS:

PHONE:

NAME:

ADDRESS:

PHONE:

NAME:

ADDRESS:

PHONE:

NAME:

ADDRESS:

PHONE:

H

NAME:

ADDRESS:

PHONE:

NAME:

ADDRESS:

PHONE:

NAME:

ADDRESS:

PHONE:

NAME:

ADDRESS:

PHONE:

NAME:

ADDRESS:

PHONE:

The Disguise of Absolute Power, 1990.
Acrylic on lounge wall paper, 48 x 31cm.
Da Souza Collection, Barcelona.

TIB's bold daubs and masterfully controlled flamboyance enables her to explore the darker side of her inner self.

I

NAME: _____

ADDRESS: _____

_____

_____

PHONE: _____

NAME: _____

ADDRESS: _____

_____

_____

PHONE: _____

NAME: _____

ADDRESS: _____

_____

_____

PHONE: _____

NAME: _____

ADDRESS: _____

_____

_____

PHONE: _____

NAME: _____

ADDRESS: _____

_____

_____

PHONE: _____

FLUFF'S works are energized by a lively confusion of elements which provide insights into canine bluff and blunder.

J

NAME: _____

ADDRESS: _____

_____

_____

PHONE: _____

NAME: _____

ADDRESS: _____

_____

_____

PHONE: _____

NAME: _____

ADDRESS: _____

_____

_____

PHONE: _____

NAME: _____

ADDRESS: _____

_____

_____

PHONE: _____

Doggone Doggy Doggerel, (detail), 1995.
Acrylic on painted lounge wall, 110 x 85 cm.
Photograph courtesy of the Joy Willis Foundation, Sydney.

NAME:

ADDRESS:

PHONE:

NAME:

ADDRESS:

PHONE:

NAME:

ADDRESS:

PHONE:

NAME:

ADDRESS:

PHONE:

NAME:

ADDRESS:

PHONE:

J

NAME:

ADDRESS:

PHONE:

NAME:

ADDRESS:

PHONE:

NAME:

ADDRESS:

PHONE:

NAME:

ADDRESS:

PHONE:

NAME:

ADDRESS:

PHONE:

K

NILDJAT, a long-eared Aswan, is similar to the temple cats of ancient Egypt who marked sacred papyrus scrolls.

NAME:

ADDRESS:

PHONE:

NAME:

ADDRESS:

PHONE:

NAME:

ADDRESS:

PHONE:

NAME:

ADDRESS:

PHONE:

Egyptian feline funerary scroll with cat paw markings, c.5000 BC. George Young Museum, Berkeley.

NAME:

ADDRESS:

PHONE:

NAME:

ADDRESS:

PHONE:

NAME:

ADDRESS:

PHONE:

NAME:

ADDRESS:

PHONE:

NAME:

ADDRESS:

PHONE:

K

NAME:

ADDRESS:

PHONE:

NAME:

ADDRESS:

PHONE:

NAME:

ADDRESS:

PHONE:

NAME:

ADDRESS:

PHONE:

NAME:

ADDRESS:

PHONE:

Wonglu, (triptych detail), 1990.
Scented acrylic on card and wall, 72 x 152cm.
Phillip Wood Gallery, Berkeley.

Wong Wong & Lu Lu (left), are duo painters who have twice won the Italian Zampa d'Oro (Golden Paw) award.

L

NAME:

ADDRESS:

PHONE:

NAME:

ADDRESS:

PHONE:

NAME:

ADDRESS:

PHONE:

NAME:

ADDRESS:

PHONE:

NAME:

ADDRESS:

PHONE:

NAME:

ADDRESS:

PHONE:

NAME:

ADDRESS:

PHONE:

NAME:

ADDRESS:

PHONE:

NAME:

ADDRESS:

PHONE:

NAME:

ADDRESS:

PHONE:

L

NAME:

ADDRESS:

PHONE:

NAME:

ADDRESS:

PHONE:

NAME:

ADDRESS:

PHONE:

NAME:

ADDRESS:

PHONE:

NAME:

ADDRESS:

PHONE:

Blue Mice Blues, 1995.
Scented acrylic on colored card, 72 x 51cm.
The Olivia David Feline Art Research Trust, N.Y.

HICKORY'S simple strokes of pigment perfectly depict the rudiments of an upward running rummage of rodents.

M

NAME:

ADDRESS:

PHONE:

NAME:

ADDRESS:

PHONE:

NAME:

ADDRESS:

PHONE:

NAME:

ADDRESS:

PHONE:

NAME:

ADDRESS:

PHONE:

NAME:

ADDRESS:

PHONE:

NAME:

ADDRESS:

PHONE:

NAME:

ADDRESS:

PHONE:

NAME:

ADDRESS:

PHONE:

NAME:

ADDRESS:

PHONE:

M

NAME:

ADDRESS:

PHONE:

NAME:

ADDRESS:

PHONE:

NAME:

ADDRESS:

PHONE:

NAME:

ADDRESS:

PHONE:

NAME:

ADDRESS:

PHONE:

NAME:

ADDRESS:

PHONE:

NAME:

ADDRESS:

PHONE:

NAME:

ADDRESS:

PHONE:

NAME:

ADDRESS:

PHONE:

NAME:

ADDRESS:

PHONE:

M

NAME:

ADDRESS:

PHONE:

NAME:

ADDRESS:

PHONE:

NAME:

ADDRESS:

PHONE:

NAME:

ADDRESS:

PHONE:

NAME:

ADDRESS:

PHONE:

Within and Beyond, (detail), 1994.
Acrylic on bathroom wall paper, 110 x 85 cm.
Preserved *in situ* at the artist's residence,
San Francisco.

SUKY's heavy use of murky purples and blues conveys an almost overwhelming sense of futility and emptiness.

N

NAME:

ADDRESS:

PHONE:

NAME:

ADDRESS:

PHONE:

NAME:

ADDRESS:

PHONE:

NAME:

ADDRESS:

PHONE:

NAME:

ADDRESS:

PHONE:

NAME:

ADDRESS:

PHONE:

NAME:

ADDRESS:

PHONE:

NAME:

ADDRESS:

PHONE:

NAME:

ADDRESS:

PHONE:

NAME:

ADDRESS:

PHONE:

NAME:

ADDRESS:

PHONE:

NAME:

ADDRESS:

PHONE:

NAME:

ADDRESS:

PHONE:

NAME:

ADDRESS:

PHONE:

NAME:

ADDRESS:

PHONE:

OEDIPUS nourishes her insights with multi-colored flicks that excite with their suggestion of avian fright and flight.

O

NAME: _____

ADDRESS: _____

_____

_____

PHONE: _____

NAME: _____

ADDRESS: _____

_____

_____

PHONE: _____

NAME: _____

ADDRESS: _____

_____

_____

PHONE: _____

NAME: _____

ADDRESS: _____

_____

_____

PHONE: _____

Oiseau To Go, 1992.
Scented acrylic paste on colored board, 67 x 43cm.
Photograph courtesy of the
Catinsky Gallery, Sausalito, California.

NAME:

ADDRESS:

PHONE:

NAME:

ADDRESS:

PHONE:

NAME:

ADDRESS:

PHONE:

NAME:

ADDRESS:

PHONE:

NAME:

ADDRESS:

PHONE:

O

NAME:

ADDRESS:

PHONE:

NAME:

ADDRESS:

PHONE:

NAME:

ADDRESS:

PHONE:

NAME:

ADDRESS:

PHONE:

NAME:

ADDRESS:

PHONE:

PRINCESS uses a combination of angled and vertical strokes which enable her to explore a wide variety of subjects.

P

NAME:

ADDRESS:

PHONE:

NAME:

ADDRESS:

PHONE:

NAME:

ADDRESS:

PHONE:

NAME:

ADDRESS:

PHONE:

Regularly Ridiculed Rodents, 1993.
Ink on paper, 52 x 83cm.
Patrick Hutchings Collection, Melbourne.

NAME:

ADDRESS:

PHONE:

NAME:

ADDRESS:

PHONE:

NAME:

ADDRESS:

PHONE:

NAME:

ADDRESS:

PHONE:

NAME:

ADDRESS:

PHONE:

P

NAME:

ADDRESS:

PHONE:

NAME:

ADDRESS:

PHONE:

NAME:

ADDRESS:

PHONE:

NAME:

ADDRESS:

PHONE:

NAME:

ADDRESS:

PHONE:

NAME:

ADDRESS:

PHONE:

NAME:

ADDRESS:

PHONE:

NAME:

ADDRESS:

PHONE:

NAME:

ADDRESS:

PHONE:

NAME:

ADDRESS:

PHONE:

P

NAME:

ADDRESS:

PHONE:

NAME:

ADDRESS:

PHONE:

NAME:

ADDRESS:

PHONE:

NAME:

ADDRESS:

PHONE:

NAME:

ADDRESS:

PHONE:

Serious Ramifications, 1992.
Acrylic on board, 73 x 62cm.
McGillicuddy Art Gallery,
Christchurch, New Zealand.

SMOKEY often uses catnip before painting, but despite this his work reflects no obvious psychedelic element.

Q

NAME:

ADDRESS:

PHONE:

NAME:

ADDRESS:

PHONE:

NAME:

ADDRESS:

PHONE:

NAME:

ADDRESS:

PHONE:

NAME:

ADDRESS:

PHONE:

Journey by See, (detail), 1992.
Acrylic on stained fence palings, 974 x 87cm.
Private collection, Bologna.

SIMKIN'S painting awakens feelings of travel and escape with its free and open leaps of color across the fence.

R

NAME:

ADDRESS:

PHONE:

NAME:

ADDRESS:

PHONE:

NAME:

ADDRESS:

PHONE:

NAME:

ADDRESS:

PHONE:

NAME:

ADDRESS:

PHONE:

NAME:

ADDRESS:

PHONE:

NAME:

ADDRESS:

PHONE:

NAME:

ADDRESS:

PHONE:

NAME:

ADDRESS:

PHONE:

NAME:

ADDRESS:

PHONE:

R

NAME:

ADDRESS:

PHONE:

NAME:

ADDRESS:

PHONE:

NAME:

ADDRESS:

PHONE:

NAME:

ADDRESS:

PHONE:

NAME:

ADDRESS:

PHONE:

RUMBLE'S works play on the motif of the attuned dog and testify to his search for some form of canine sensitivity.

S

NAME:

ADDRESS:

PHONE:

NAME:

ADDRESS:

PHONE:

NAME:

ADDRESS:

PHONE:

NAME:

ADDRESS:

PHONE:

Thin-legged Dog Sniffing Spring Flowers Perhaps, 1996.
Acrylic on colored card, 73 x 49cm.
British Council for the Promotion of Feline Aesthetics.

NAME:

ADDRESS:

PHONE:

NAME:

ADDRESS:

PHONE:

NAME:

ADDRESS:

PHONE:

NAME:

ADDRESS:

PHONE:

NAME:

ADDRESS:

PHONE:

S

NAME:

ADDRESS:

PHONE:

NAME:

ADDRESS:

PHONE:

NAME:

ADDRESS:

PHONE:

NAME:

ADDRESS:

PHONE:

NAME:

ADDRESS:

PHONE:

NAME:

ADDRESS:

PHONE:

NAME:

ADDRESS:

PHONE:

NAME:

ADDRESS:

PHONE:

NAME:

ADDRESS:

PHONE:

NAME:

ADDRESS:

PHONE:

S

NAME:

ADDRESS:

PHONE:

NAME:

ADDRESS:

PHONE:

NAME:

ADDRESS:

PHONE:

NAME:

ADDRESS:

PHONE:

NAME:

ADDRESS:

PHONE:

CHISKKA, a circus cat in Latvia, was liberated in 1989 after being exploited as a performing painter for seven years.

T

NAME:

ADDRESS:

PHONE:

NAME:

ADDRESS:

PHONE:

NAME:

ADDRESS:

PHONE:

NAME:

ADDRESS:

PHONE:

Mrs. Broadmoore's Amazing Painting Cat, c.1887.
Lithograph, Museum of Animal Acts, Wisconsin.

NAME:

ADDRESS:

PHONE:

NAME:

ADDRESS:

PHONE:

NAME:

ADDRESS:

PHONE:

NAME:

ADDRESS:

PHONE:

NAME:

ADDRESS:

PHONE:

T

NAME:

ADDRESS:

PHONE:

NAME:

ADDRESS:

PHONE:

NAME:

ADDRESS:

PHONE:

NAME:

ADDRESS:

PHONE:

NAME:

ADDRESS:

PHONE:

NAME:

ADDRESS:

PHONE:

NAME:

ADDRESS:

PHONE:

NAME:

ADDRESS:

PHONE:

NAME:

ADDRESS:

PHONE:

NAME:

ADDRESS:

PHONE:

T

NAME:

ADDRESS:

PHONE:

NAME:

ADDRESS:

PHONE:

NAME:

ADDRESS:

PHONE:

NAME:

ADDRESS:

PHONE:

NAME:

ADDRESS:

PHONE:

BISCUIT's lively forms, painted on corrugated iron, suggest birds (crows & larks?) flocking over green undulating hills.

U

NAME:

ADDRESS:

PHONE:

NAME:

ADDRESS:

PHONE:

NAME:

ADDRESS:

PHONE:

NAME:

ADDRESS:

PHONE:

Hills, Bills, Trills & Kills, (detail), 1996.
Acrylic on painted corrugated iron fence, 480 x 89cm.
Preserved *in situ*, Stanford University, California.

Whirling Dogs on a False Lead to Nowhere,
(detail), 1989. Acrylic on colored card, 58 x 37cm.
Private collection, Singapore.

BIGBIT's dramatic sweeps of color display a bold (possibly misguided) utopian striving for a dog-free urban ethic.

V

NAME:

ADDRESS:

PHONE:

NAME:

ADDRESS:

PHONE:

NAME:

ADDRESS:

PHONE:

NAME:

ADDRESS:

PHONE:

NAME:

ADDRESS:

PHONE:

MARMADUKE'S vivid studies are well known in Holland where they sell at auction for more than $15,000 each.

W

NAME:

ADDRESS:

PHONE:

NAME:

ADDRESS:

PHONE:

NAME:

ADDRESS:

PHONE:

NAME:

ADDRESS:

PHONE:

Midnight Tulip Tiptoe, 1995.
Acrylic on painted wall, 89 x 56cm.
Dr Karl-Heinz Petzler Feline Art Trust, Amsterdam.

NAME:

ADDRESS:

PHONE:

NAME:

ADDRESS:

PHONE:

NAME:

ADDRESS:

PHONE:

NAME:

ADDRESS:

PHONE:

NAME:

ADDRESS:

PHONE:

W

NAME:

ADDRESS:

PHONE:

NAME:

ADDRESS:

PHONE:

NAME:

ADDRESS:

PHONE:

NAME:

ADDRESS:

PHONE:

NAME:

ADDRESS:

PHONE:

NAME:

ADDRESS:

PHONE:

NAME:

ADDRESS:

PHONE:

NAME:

ADDRESS:

PHONE:

NAME:

ADDRESS:

PHONE:

NAME:

ADDRESS:

PHONE:

W

NAME:

ADDRESS:

PHONE:

NAME:

ADDRESS:

PHONE:

NAME:

ADDRESS:

PHONE:

NAME:

ADDRESS:

PHONE:

NAME:

ADDRESS:

PHONE:

Hello Dolly, 1991.
Scented acrylic on glass, 78 x 53cm.
Photograph courtesy of the American Council
for the Promotion of Non-Primate Art.

RUSTY gives his bold impression of a Russian doll further detail by adding fine scratches to the dried paint.

X

NAME:

ADDRESS:

PHONE:

NAME:

ADDRESS:

PHONE:

NAME:

ADDRESS:

PHONE:

NAME:

ADDRESS:

PHONE:

NAME:

ADDRESS:

PHONE:

Polemic Police, 1991.
Acrylic on colored card, 28 x 22 cm.
Collection of the Artist, Seattle.

Y

MAO'S Post-Minimalist soft paw–hard background contrasts, become metaphors for feline freedom and detention.

NAME:

ADDRESS:

PHONE:

NAME:

ADDRESS:

PHONE:

NAME:

ADDRESS:

PHONE:

NAME:

ADDRESS:

PHONE:

NAME:

ADDRESS:

PHONE:

LUCY'S dramatic daubs are cleverly offset by finer, more dispersed structures, at once evocative of a fluttering rondo.

Z

NAME:
ADDRESS:

PHONE:

NAME:
ADDRESS:

PHONE:

NAME:
ADDRESS:

PHONE:

NAME:
ADDRESS:

PHONE:

Balalaika Butterflies, (detail), 1995.
Acrylic on colored card, 44 x 28cm.
NZ Ailurophiles Art Association, Wellington.

TEN SPEED PRESS
P.O. Box 7123,
Berkeley, California 94707

Library of Congress Catalog information is on file with the publisher.

ISBN 0 - 89815 - 858 - 3

Published with the assistance of the American Council
for the Promotion of Non-Primate Art.

Cover illustration:
MAX, *Birdies,* (detail), 1991. Acrylic paste on painted wall. 86 x 130cm. Private collection

Frontispiece:
ORANGELLO, *Beam Me Up*, 1982. Acrylic on yellow card, 48 x 68cm.
Phillip Wood Gallery, Berkeley.

First printing 1996

Printed and bound in China

1 2 3 4 5 - 00 99 98 97 96